# PARIS WALKS

## Europe Made Easy
Travel Guides

www.eatndrink.com

Text and Maps Copyright © 2018 by Andy Herbach
- All Rights Reserved -
ISBN-13: 978-1721624126
ISBN-10: 1721624120

The author has made every effort to be as accurate as possible, but neither he nor the publisher assumes responsibility for the services provided by any business listed in this guide; for any errors or omissions; or any loss, damage, or disruptions in your travels for any reason.

### ABOUT THE AUTHOR

Andy Herbach is the author of the *Eating & Drinking* series of menu translators and restaurant guides, including *Eating & Drinking in Paris*, *Eating & Drinking in Italy*, *Eating & Drinking in Spain and Portugal*, and *Eating & Drinking in Latin America*. He is also the author of several travel guides, including *Europe Made Easy*, *Paris Made Easy*, *Amsterdam Made Easy*, *Berlin Made Easy*, *Barcelona Made Easy*, and *Open Road's Best of the French Riviera and Provence*. Andy is a lawyer and resides in Palm Springs, California.

You can e-mail him corrections, additions, and comments at eatndrink@aol.com or through his website at www.eatndrink.com.

# Table of Contents

**1. Introduction**  7

**2. Overview**  9

**3. Itineraries**  18

**4. Paris Walks**  21
Islands Walk  21
Left Bank Walk  26
Marais Walk  31
Major Sights Walk  36
Montmartre Walk  42
Culinary Walks  46

**5. Practical Matters**  49
Getting to Paris  49
  Airports/Arrival  49
Getting Around Paris  50
  Car Rental  50
  Métro (Subway)  50
  Buses  51
  Taxis  51
Basic Information  51
  Banking and Changing Money  51
  Business Hours  51
  Climate and Weather  52
  Consulates and Embassies  52
  Electricity  52
  Emergencies and Safety  52
  Insurance  52
  Festivals  53
  Holidays  54
  Internet Access  55
  Language  55

Packing   55
Passport Regulations   55
Postal Services   56
Restrooms   56
Smoking   56
Telephones   57
Time   57
Tipping   57
Tourist Information   58
Water   58
Web Sites   58
Essential Phrases   59

## Maps

Major Sights (Central Paris)   10-11
Arrondissements   13
Major Sights (West)   14
Major Sights (East)   15
Montmartre Sights   16
Islands Walk   22
Left Bank Walk   27
Marais Walk   32
Major Sights Walk   38-39
Montmartre Walk   43

# Reviews for travel guides by Andy Herbach
•

*"...an opinionated little compendium."*
Eating & Drinking in Paris
- New York Times

*"Everything you need to devour Paris on the quick."*
Best of Paris
- Chicago Tribune

*"an elegant, small guide..."*
Eating & Drinking in Italy
- Minneapolis Star Tribune

*"Makes dining easy and enjoyable."*
Eating & Drinking in Spain
- Toronto Sun

*"Guide illuminates the City of Light."*
Wining & Dining in Paris
- Newsday

*"This handy pocket guide is all you need..."*
Paris Made Easy
- France Magazine

*"Small enough for discreet use..."*
Eating & Drinking in Paris
- USA Today

*"It's written as if a friend were talking to you."*
Eating & Drinking in Italy
- Celebrity Chef Tyler Florence

# 1. Introduction

**Paris** is the most fabulous city in the world, not because of the Eiffel Tower or the Champs-Élysées, but because there's simply no other place in the world like it ...

# 8 PARIS WALKS

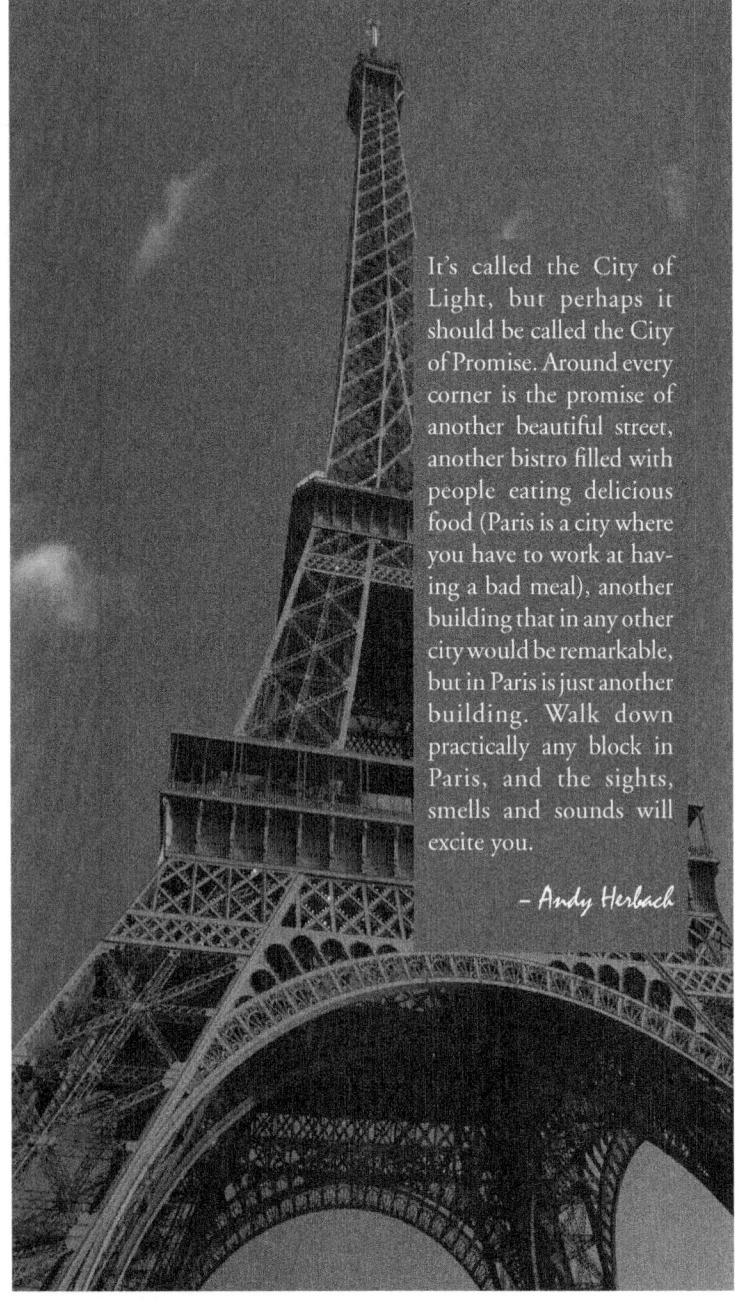

It's called the City of Light, but perhaps it should be called the City of Promise. Around every corner is the promise of another beautiful street, another bistro filled with people eating delicious food (Paris is a city where you have to work at having a bad meal), another building that in any other city would be remarkable, but in Paris is just another building. Walk down practically any block in Paris, and the sights, smells and sounds will excite you.

– *Andy Herbach*

## 2. Overview

Paris is a large metropolis, home to millions. Sure, it's a city where people live and work, but in Paris, they carry *baguettes*, stop at sidewalk cafés, and have a leisurely cup of coffee or glass of wine.

If you have only **a short time in Paris**, I'll make it easy for you to truly experience the city. You'll find helpful walks through the most interesting areas of the city in this little guide.

Take great museums (like the Musée d'Orsay), amazing monuments (like the Eiffel Tower), historic churches (like Notre-Dame), fantastic neighborhoods (like the Marais) and excellent French cuisine and you've got the ingredients for **a great trip to Paris**.

Paris is divided into 20 arrondissements or districts, each with its own city hall, police station, post office and mayor.

### Islands
The Île de la Cité is the birthplace of Paris. Surrounded by the Seine River, this island is home to Notre-Dame, Ste-Chapelle and the Conciergerie. The Île St-Louis is a charming residential island.

### 1st and 2nd Arrondissements
The 1st is the center of Paris where many tourist attractions are found, including the Louvre, Palais Royal and Jardin des Tuileries. The adjoining 2nd is primarily a business district.

### 3rd and 4th Arrondissements
The Marais is comprised of roughly the 3rd and 4th arrondissements on the Right Bank. This area, with its small streets and beautiful squares, is filled with interesting shops. It's home to both a thriving Jewish community and a large gay community. It's considered the "cœur historique," historic heart of Paris, and has retained some of the flavor of the French Renaissance.

# 10 PARIS WALKS

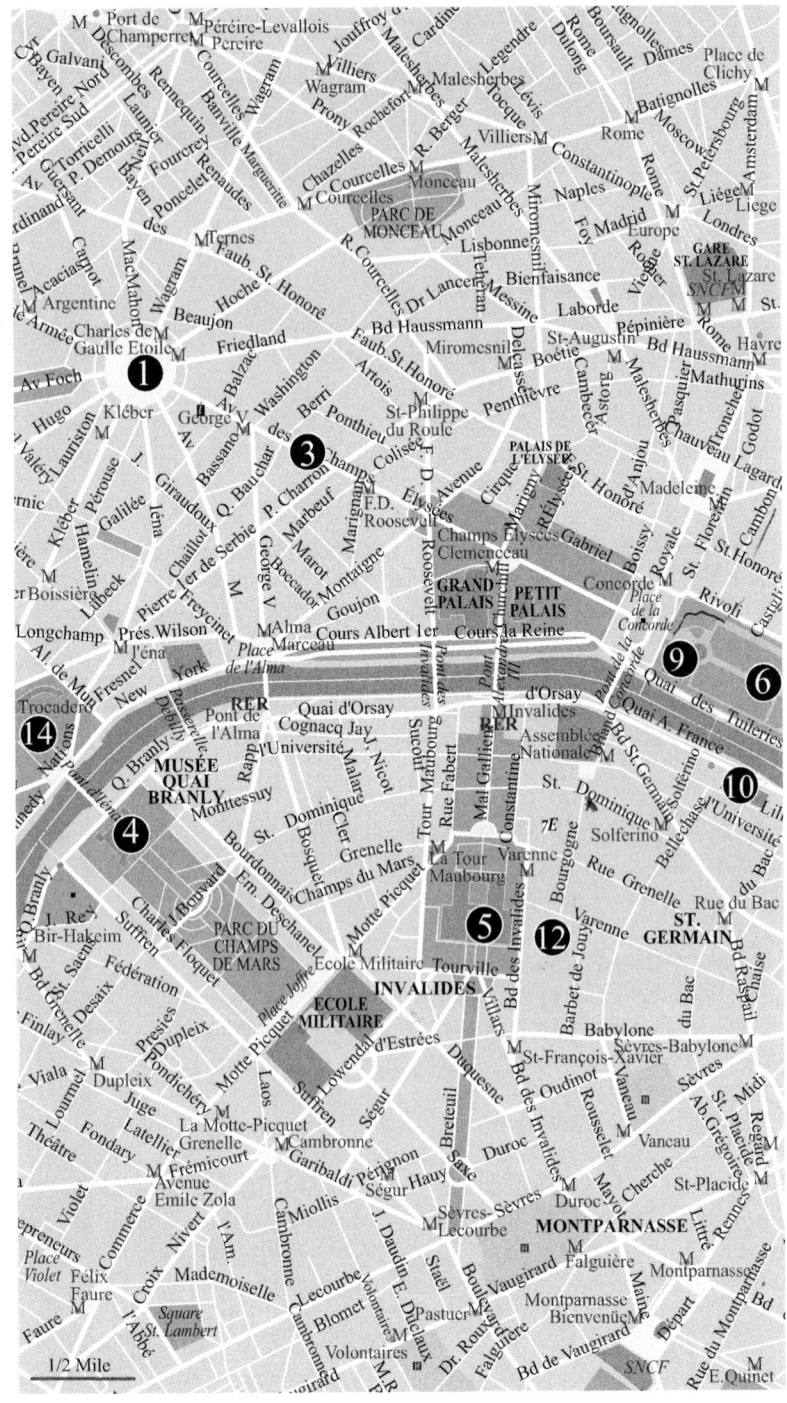

# 11 OVERVIEW

A - Makamava Café

## Major Sights
1. Arc de Triomphe
2. Centre Pompidou
3. Champs-Élysées
4. Eiffel, Tour
5. Hôtel des Invalides
6. Jardin des Tuileries
7. Jardin du Luxembourg
8. Louvre
9. Musée de l'Orangerie
10. Musée d'Orsay
11. Musée Picasso
12. Musée Rodin
13. Notre-Dame
14. Palais de Chaillot
15. Palais Royal
16. place des Vosges
17. Sacré-Coeur
18. Ste-Chapelle

M Métro Stop

# Paris Arrondissements
## *Major Sights Maps*

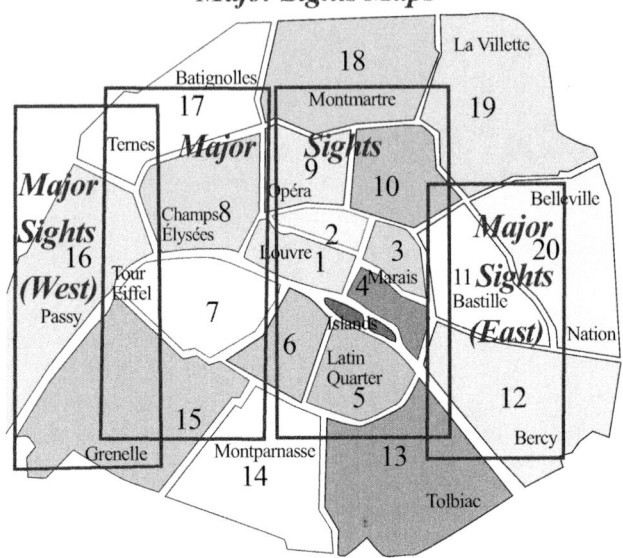

### 5th and 6th Arrondissements
The 5th and 6th, south of Île de la Cité on the Left Bank of the Seine, is home to the Quartier Latin (Latin Quarter). It's a maze of small streets and squares surrounding La Sorbonne, the famous university. The name Latin Quarter comes from the university tradition of speaking and studying in Latin.

### 7th Arrondissement
The chic 7th is home to some of the city's grandest sights, including the Eiffel Tower, Musée d'Orsay and Les Invalides.

### 8th and 16th Arrondissements
Luxurious shopping, the place de la Concorde, the Champs-Élysées and the Arc de Triomphe are all found in the 8th. In the adjoining 16th, you'll find upscale shopping, elegant residences and parks such as the Trocadéro.

### 9th Arrondissement
Home to the opulent Opéra Garnier, a center for shopping (most major department stores are here), and a mecca for nightlife.

## 10th Arrondissement
Home to two great train stations, the Gare du Nord and Gare de l'Est. It wasn't too long ago that guidebooks didn't even mention the 10th. Today, this working-class area is increasingly popular with artists, making for an interesting mix. Boutiques, cafés, galleries and trendy restaurants seem to have multiplied overnight, especially near the Canal St-Martin.

## 11th Arrondissement
The 11th, centered on the Bastille, is primarily a residential area that has become increasingly hip lately, especially around rue de Charonne and rue de Lappe. Great restaurants!

## 12th Arrondissement
The 12th is home to the Gare de Lyon train station. This primarily residential area is bordered on the east by the Bois de Vincennes, a beautiful park.

## 13th Arrondissement
The 13th is a residential area, home to Chinatown and the grand National Library.

## 14th and 15th Arrondissements
Known as Montparnasse and centered around the lively boulevard Montparnasse (once the center of Paris's avant-garde scene), these areas are primarily residential.

## 17th Arrondissement
The Arc de Triomphe and beautiful Parc Monceau border the residential 17th.

## 18th Arrondissement
Once a small village of vineyards and windmills, Montmartre is dominated by the massive Sacred Heart Basilica. It's also home to the sleazy place Pigalle and the largest flea market in Paris.

## 19th Arrondissement
Diverse residential area, home to the futuristic Parc de la Villette.

## 20th Arrondissement
Dominated by the Cimetière du Père-Lachaise. Another diverse neighborhood.

14 PARIS WALKS

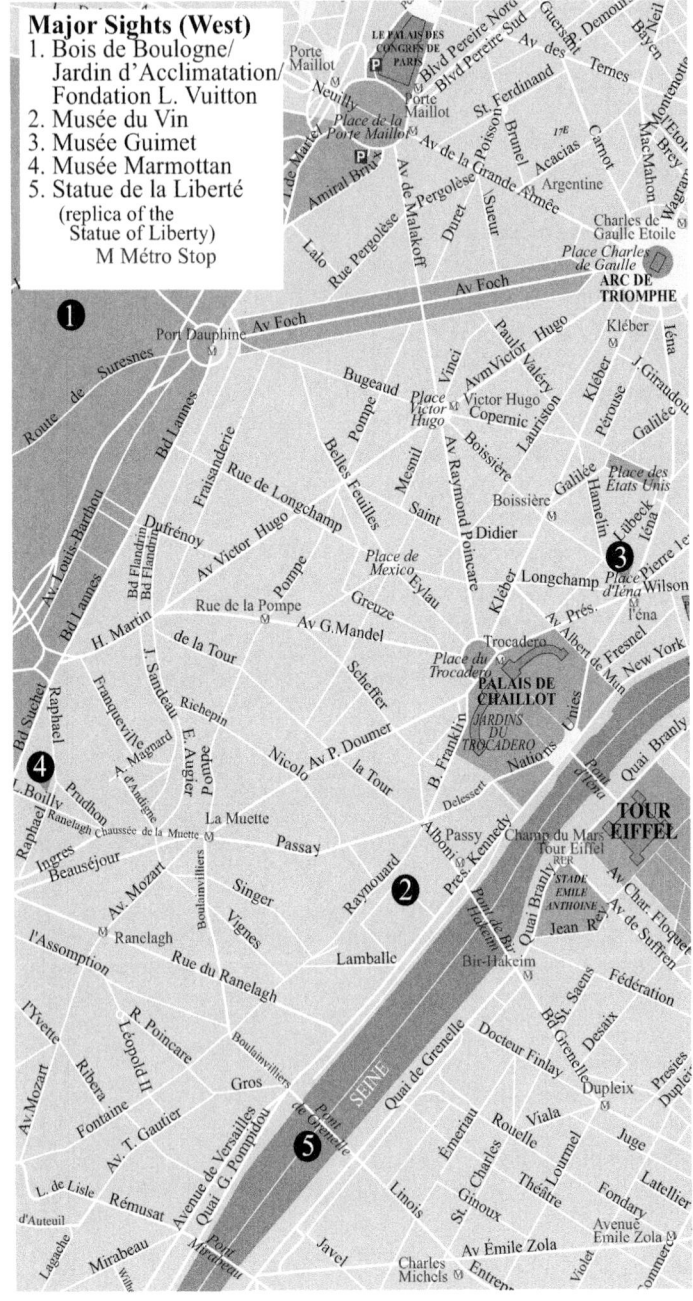

15 OVERVIEW

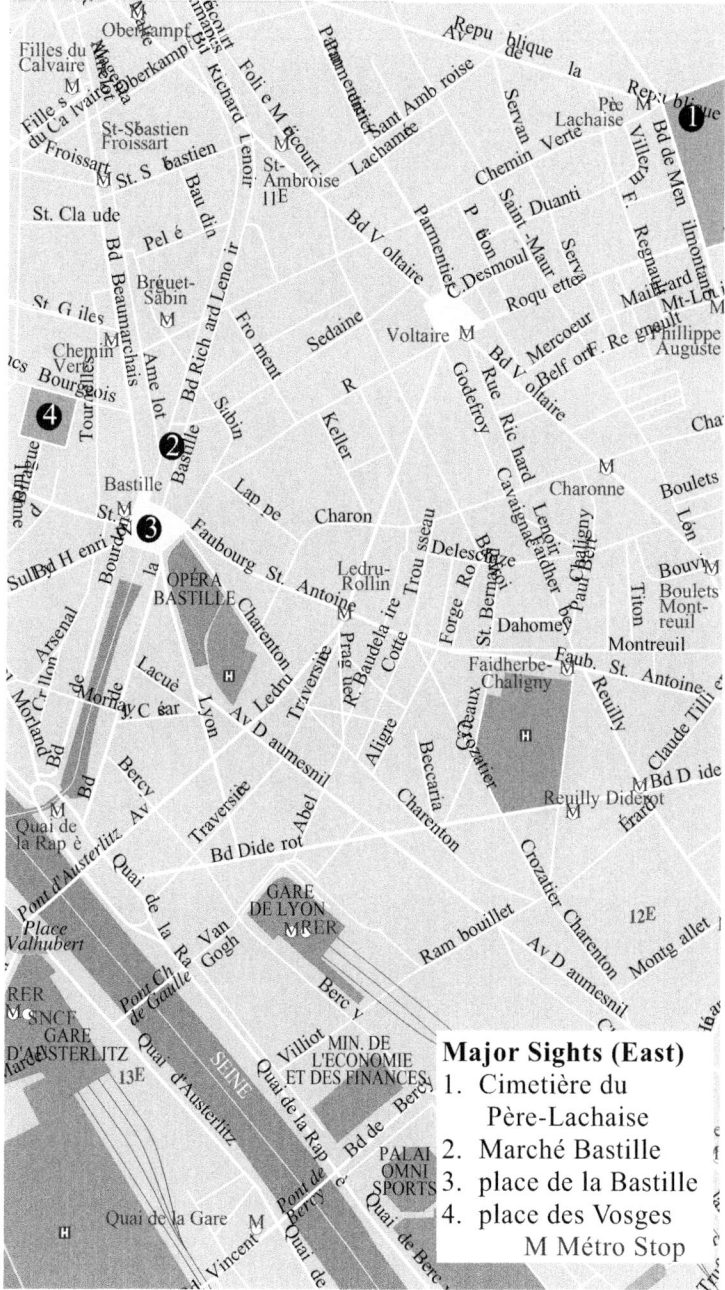

**Major Sights (East)**
1. Cimetière du Père-Lachaise
2. Marché Bastille
3. place de la Bastille
4. place des Vosges
   M Métro Stop

16 PARIS WALKS

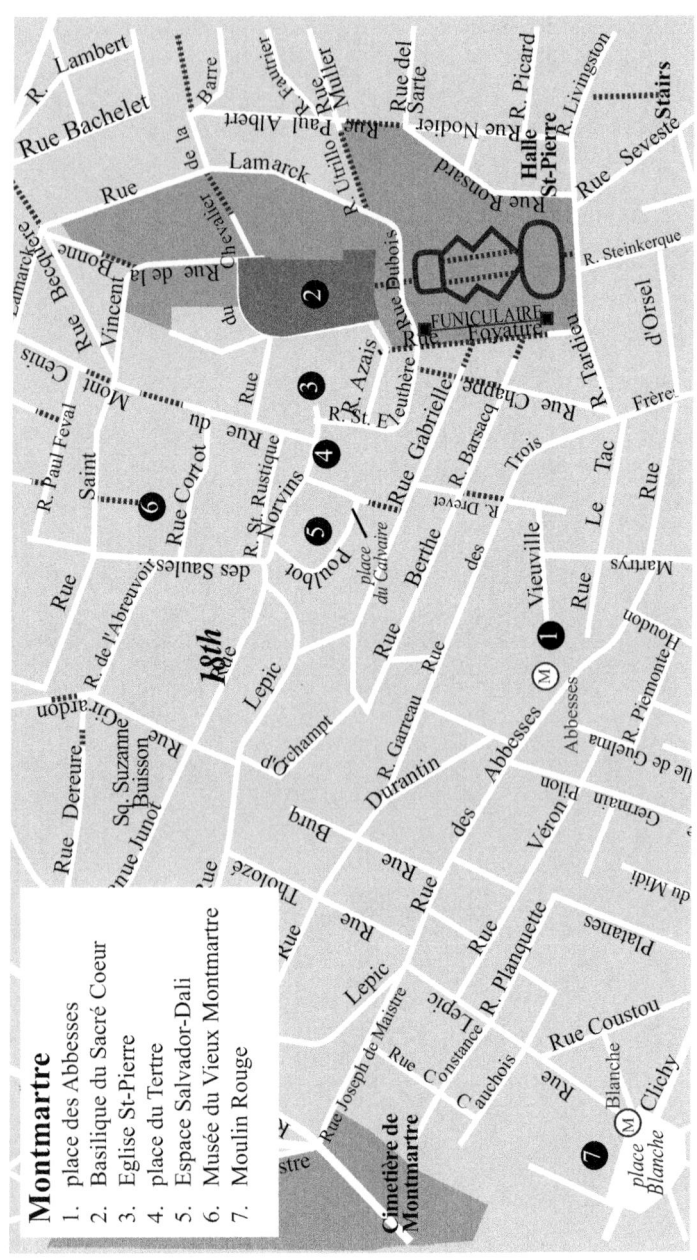

**Montmartre**
1. place des Abbesses
2. Basilique du Sacré Coeur
3. Eglise St-Pierre
4. place du Tertre
5. Espace Salvador-Dali
6. Musée du Vieux Montmartre
7. Moulin Rouge

17 OVERVIEW

**Finding an Address**
**Address numbers** begin at the Seine River for north-south streets. East-west addresses run parallel to the river (following the course of the river). Street signs aren't like at home. They are at the corner of the street, but usually on a plaque attached to the building, way above eye level.

**Best Neighborhoods**
- the **Marais**, the historic heart of Paris
- **St-Germain-des-Prés**, filled with upscale galleries, boutiques and restaurants
- the narrow, winding streets of **Montmartre**
- **Montorgueil**, a lively quarter where diverse shops line the pedestrian streets

# 3. Itineraries

These are my suggestions for three fabulous days in Paris!

**Day One: A day on the Left Bank**
**Morning**: Visit a typical Parisian café. You can find one on nearly every street. Why don't you start by having coffee and a *croissant*? If you order *un café*, you'll get a small cup of very strong black coffee. If you'd like a larger cup of coffee with steamed milk, ask for *un crème*.

**Sights**: Explore the **Musée d'Orsay** (closed Tuesday), a magnificent museum, and so much more manageable than the Louvre.

**Walk**: Discover the Left Bank by taking the **Left Bank Walk** (*see our Walks chapter*). You can have a glass of wine at one of the many cafés along the way.

**Dinner**: Head to one of the great Left Bank restaurants found in our guide *Eating & Drinking in Paris*.

**Evening**: After dinner, head to **Café Marly** at 93 rue de Rivoli (1st/ Métro Palais Royal-Musée d'Orsay). You'll pay for the view overlooking the pyramid entrance to the Louvre (*see photo at left*), but it's a great place to end your day with a glass of champagne. How French!

ITINERARIES 19

Day Two: The Islands and the Marais
**Sights**: Head to the islands in the middle of the Seine River and visit **Notre-Dame** and the **Deportation Memorial**.

**Walk**: The Marais neighborhood, with its small streets and beautiful squares, is filled with interesting shops and plenty of places for lunch. It's considered the historic heart of Paris. To experience it, take the **Marais Walk**.

**Dinner**: Dine at one of the great Right Bank restaurants found in our guide *Eating & Drinking in Paris*.

**Evening**: End your day by heading to the **Seine River**. Walk along the river, taking in the elegantly lit **Notre-Dame** and the stunning beauty of this amazing city.

Day Three: Major Sights
**Morning**: Start your day in the lovely **Jardin des Tuileries**. While here, stop at one of the cafés in the park, for a *croissant* and cup of coffee.

**Walk**: Take the **Major Sights Walk** in this book (including the **Arc de Triomphe** and the **Champs-Élysées**). Although it starts at the Eiffel Tower, don't wait in line to see it. You'll do that later. There are plenty of places to have a snack along the walk.

**Wine**: Duck into any one of the **Nicolas** wine shops scattered throughout the city. You'll find a selection of French wines to choose to take back to your hotel and enjoy before dinner.

**Dinner**: Wine and dine at one of the restaurants, bistros, or wine bars listed in our guide *Eating & Drinking in Paris*.

**Evening**: After dinner visit the **Eiffel Tower**. The lines will be short, the view memorable, and the light show on the hour is spectacular. There's no better way to end your day!

# 4. Paris Walks

*The real reason the French are thin ...*

The French have two-hour lunches with lots of wine and dinners that include dishes smothered with delicious cream sauces, even more wine and sinful desserts. So why are they so thin?

It's simple: **They walk everywhere**. To the market, to the cinema and yes, to the bistro. Now, you too can travel to Paris, eat and drink all you want and (hopefully!) not gain a pound. All you have to do is venture out on the walks in this chapter.

Go ahead, eat like the French. Then, refer to this chapter and get your exercise – and see the best Paris has to offer!


### ISLANDS WALK
**Approximate distance**: two miles. **Highlights**: Notre-Dame, Ste-Chapelle and Île St-Louis.

*Your walk begins by taking the métro to the Pont Neuf stop.*

You'll be in front of **La Samaritaine** department store at 19 rue de la Monnaie (closed for renovations).

*Head east along the Seine River.*

Along the river on quai de la Mégisserie (between rue des Bourdonnais and place du Châtelet) you can wander through beautiful **plant stores** and **pet shops** (birds, puppies, fish, roosters, you name it) that spill out onto the sidewalks. You'll love this little strip of Paris.

When you reach **place du Châtelet**, take in the **Fountain of the Palms**. It was ordered by Napoléon to commemorate his victories in Egypt.

22 PARIS WALKS

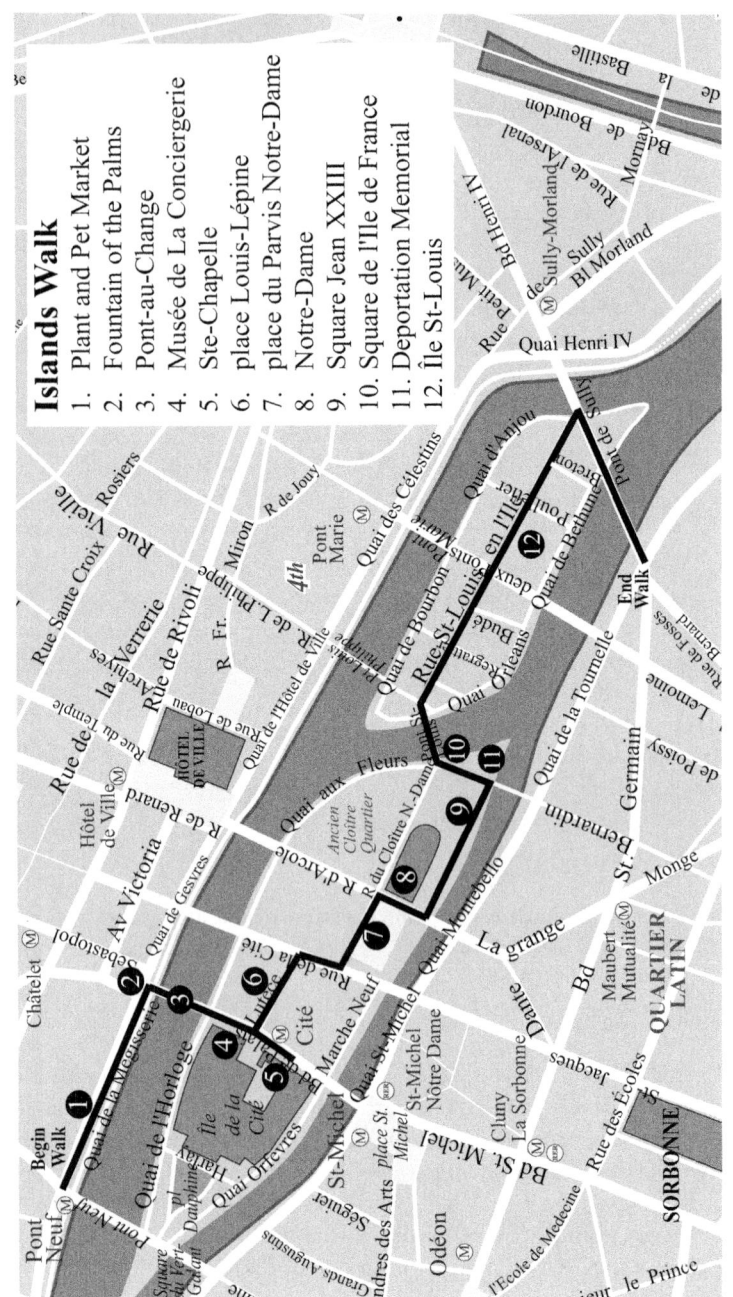

**Islands Walk**

1. Plant and Pet Market
2. Fountain of the Palms
3. Pont-au-Change
4. Musée de La Conciergerie
5. Ste-Chapelle
6. place Louis-Lépine
7. place du Parvis Notre-Dame
8. Notre-Dame
9. Square Jean XXIII
10. Square de l'Ile de France
11. Deportation Memorial
12. Île St-Louis

*Turn to your right and cross the bridge.*

The **Pont-au-Change** got its name because moneychangers used to have their booths on this bridge crossing the Seine River.

*On the other side of the Pont-au-Change is the boulevard du Palais.*

On the corner, look up and you'll see a fabulous 1334 Baroque **clock tower** (it still works), the first public clock in Paris. You're now on the **Île de la Cité**, an island in the Seine River.

*Continue down the boulevard du Palais.*

On your right is the entrance to the **Musée de la Conciergerie**, a 14th-century prison where over 2,600 people waited to have their heads chopped off, including Marie-Antoinette, during the French revolution's "Reign of Terror." If you have limited time, skip this museum and head down the street.

The Gothic palace that houses this museum along with the massive **Palais de Justice** were once part of the Palais de la Cité, the home of French kings. Today, it's home to the city's courts of law. You can watch the courts in session and view its beautiful interior for free. Closed on Sunday.

*As you pass the gates to the palace, on your right, you'll see the entrance to our next stop.*

If it's a sunny day, you cannot miss **la Ste-Chapelle**. You'll be dazzled by nearly 6,600 square feet of stained glass at this Gothic masterpiece. The walls are almost entirely stained glass. Fifteen windows depict biblical scenes from the Garden of Eden to the Apocalypse (the large rose window). The chapel was built in 1246 to house what some believe to be the Crown of Thorns, a nail from the crucifixion and other relics.

*Cross the boulevard du Palais to rue de Lutèce.*

Soon you'll see, to your left, the curvy, Art Nouveau Cité métro stop. You're now in the **place Louis-Lépine**. To your left is the lovely **Marché aux Fleurs** (flower market). On Sundays, the market becomes the **Marché aux Oiseaux** (bird market) where all types of birds, supplies and cages are sold.

*Continue on and turn right at rue de la Cité.*

Head down rue de la Cité to **place du Parvis Notre-Dame** (the square in front of Notre-Dame). It's recently been renamed Parvis Notre-Dame/place Jean-Paul-II. It's the center of all of France. The bronze plaque on the ground outside the cathedral is "Point Zéro" from which all distances in France are measured. You'll also find the entry to the **Crypte Archéologique** here with ruins of Roman Paris. Head into **Notre-Dame** and admire this incredible structure.

It's so huge that it can accommodate over 6,000 visitors. The interior is dominated by three beautiful (and immense) rose windows, and has a 7,800-pipe organ. Inside along the walls are individual chapels dedicated to saints. The most famous chapel is that of Joan of Arc in the right transept. The treasury houses relics, manuscripts and religious garments. You may want to climb the 387 steps of the north tower for a grand view of Paris. You'll also have a great view of the cathedral's famous gargoyles.

*As you exit the cathedral (with the cathedral to your back) head left and then make a left turn before the bridge.*

Stroll through **Square Jean XXIII** along the river. Behind the cathedral is the lovely **Square de l'Île de France**. Here you'll notice the "flying buttresses" that support Notre-

Dame. From these squares, take in the beauty of Paris along the Seine River.

*Directly behind the cathedral, cross the street (quai Archevêché) and head through the gate.*

You'll now enter the **Mémorial des Martyrs Français de la Déportation de 1945** (Deportation Memorial). It will take you only a short time to walk through this free memorial built in honor of the more than 30,000 citizens who were placed on boats at this spot for deportation to concentration camps. You descend steps and become surrounded by walls. Single-file, you enter a chamber. A hallway is covered with 200,000 crystals (one for each French citizen who died). At the far end of the hall is the eternal flame of hope. Don't miss this memorial. It's both moving and disturbing.

*As you leave the memorial, exit out the gate, turn right on quai Archevêché. Head to the pedestrian bridge. Take a right onto the bridge.*

You are now on the **Pont St-Louis**. There almost always are street musicians playing jazz to a crowd of onlookers.

*Continue across this bridge to the Île St-Louis.*

The **Île St-Louis** is a residential island within the city, often swamped with tourists during high season. The vast majority of the buildings on this island date back to the 1600s, making for a beautiful place to stroll, especially the small side streets. There are interesting shops and several good restaurants.

After you cross the bridge you'll be on the narrow **rue St-Louis-en-l'Île**, one of the most beautiful streets in all of Paris. A few highlights on this street are:

- No. 78: **Boulangerie St-Louis**. A great bakery.
- No. 51: **Kabrousse**. A great photo-op as the flowers spill out onto the sidewalk.

- No. 31: **Berthillon**. The best-known ice-cream shop in Paris.
- No. 19: **Eglise St-Louis-en-l'Île**. Visit the beautiful ornate interior of this church.

*At the end of the street, turn right and cross the bridge.*

This bridge (**Pont Sully**) dates back to 1874 and is actually two independent steel bridges that extend from the Île St-Louis to either side of the river. As you cross the bridge you will be treated to a wonderful view of one of the sights you have just visited, Notre-Dame. You're now on the Left Bank and can continue down the famous boulevard St-Germain-des-Prés.

*You can head back to your hotelf rom any number of métro stops along the boulevard St-Germain-des-Prés.*

### LEFT BANK WALK

**Approximate distance**: two-and-a-half miles. **Highlights**: Musée Maillol, St-Germain-des-Prés, and the Jardin du Luxembourg. Musée Maillol is closed on Tuesday.

*Take the métro to the rue du Bac stop.*

When you get out of the métro, you'll be at the crossroads of rue du Bac, boulevard Raspail and boulevard St-Germain-des-Prés. On the corner is a typical Parisian café, the **Café St-Germain**. Why don't you start by having coffee and a croissant here? If you order *un café*, you'll get a small cup of very strong black coffee. If you'd like a larger cup of coffee with steamed milk, ask for *un crème*.

After you've had your wonderful Parisian coffee, you're going to visit one of the most interesting, if not the most bizarre, shops in Paris.

*Cross rue Raspail and boulevard St-Germain-des-Prés to rue du Bac.*

At 46 rue du Bac you'll find **Deyrolle**, a taxidermy shop "stuffed" with everything from snakes to baby elephants to zebras. Also on display are collections of butterflies, shells and minerals from all over the world. Kids seem to love this place. You have to go upstairs! The shop also sells planters, clothes and other household items (some modeled on the stuffed animals). Very quirky! It's closed on Sunday.

WALKS 27

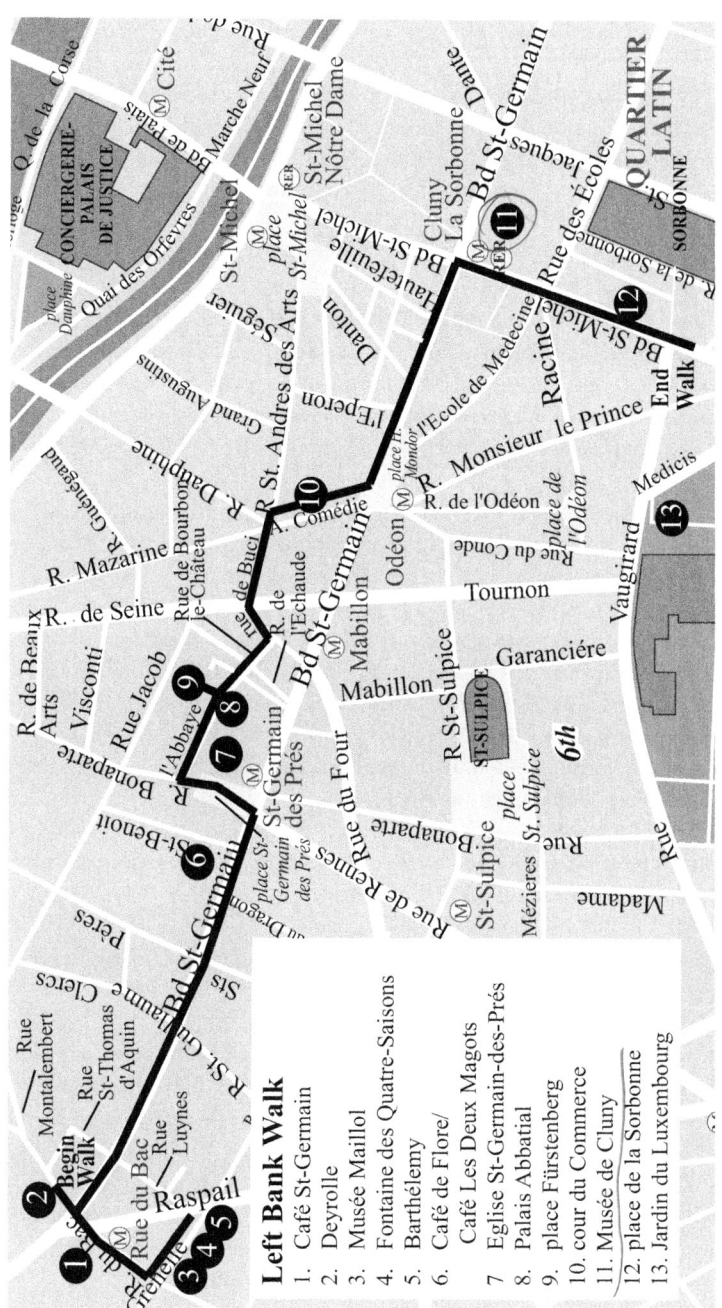

### Left Bank Walk
1. Café St-Germain
2. Deyrolle
3. Musée Maillol
4. Fontaine des Quatre-Saisons
5. Barthélemy
6. Café de Flore/Café Les Deux Magots
7. Eglise St-Germain-des-Prés
8. Palais Abbatial
9. place Fürstenberg
10. cour du Commerce
11. Musée de Cluny
12. place de la Sorbonne
13. Jardin du Luxembourg

*Head back toward the café and up rue de Bac in the opposite direction.*

On this short block, you'll find everything from a butcher shop to a fish shop, and an attractive antique shop called **Magnolia**. Notice that horse head above the butcher shop on your left? That means that the store still sells horse meat.

*When you get to rue de Grenelle, make a left.*

As you head down rue de Grenelle, you can stop at the **Musée Maillol** (Fondation Dina Vierny-Musée Maillol) at 61. The works of Aristide Maillol, a contemporary of Matisse, are here, along with rare sketches by Picasso, Cézanne, Degas and other 20th-century artists. The museum also features important exhibits.

Next to the museum is the **Fontaine des Quatre-Saisons**, completed in 1745. It's decorated with figures representing the four seasons (and a few cherubs thrown in for good measure).

Cheese is like gold to the French. Charles de Gaulle is reported to have said, "How can anyone govern a nation that has 246 different kinds of cheese?" At number 51 is **Barthélemy**, a small, popular cheese shop. You'll know when you're getting close as you'll be able to smell it. When you walk in, you're overtaken by the intense smell of some of the best cheeses available in France. Closed Sunday and Monday.

*Backtrack to the café (down rue de Grenelle to rue du Bac). Turn right onto boulevard St-Germain-des-Prés. Walk down the left side of this famous boulevard.*

At 218 is **Madeleine Gely**, a shop that's been making handmade umbrellas since 1834.

You have not experienced Paris unless you visit one of its many cafés. **Café de Flore** is at 172 boulevard St-Germain-des-Prés. Just a few steps away is **Café Les Deux Magots** at 6 place St-Germain-des-Prés. Great people-watching at both of these famous cafés.

Between Café Les Deux Magots and Café de Flore is **La Hune**, at 170 boulevard St-Germain. This incredible bookstore is packed until midnight. There's an extensive architecture-and-art section upstairs.

*Take a left at place St-Germain-des-Prés.*

Stop into the **Eglise St-Germain-des-Prés**. This church dates back to the 6th century. A Gothic choir, 19th-century spire and Romanesque paintings all attest to its long history.

*As you exit the church, head right and then turn right onto rue de l'Abbaye.*

On the right side of rue de l'Abbaye is the rose-colored 17th-century **Palais Abbatial**.

*Take a left into place Fürstenberg.*

At the center of **place Fürstenberg** is a white-globed lamppost. Look familiar? This scenic square has been seen in many films. It's often filled with street musicians, some of them surprisingly good.

*Head back to rue de l'Abbaye and continue down the street which turns into rue de Bourbon-le-Château.*

On the corner is a wonderful wine shop, **La Dernière Goutte**.

*Take a left on the attractive rue de Buci.*

On rue de Buci, you'll pass along small cafés and interesting shops on a mostly pedestrian street. At the intersection of rue de Buci and rue St-André-des-Arts, you'll find a typical French outdoor market at certain times of the day.

*Rue de Buci turns into rue St-André-des-Arts. Take a right at 61.*

The **cour du Commerce** is a cobblestone alleyway off of la rue St-André-des-Arts, which is lined with wonderful shops and restaurants. Benjamin Franklin is said to have frequented **Procope**, the oldest *brasserie* in Paris.

*At the end of the passageway, turn left and you'll be back on boulevard St-Germain. Continue on this street and take a right onto boulevard St-Michel.*

On your left at the intersection is the **Musée de Cluny** (Musée National du Moyen Age/Thermes de Cluny) at 6 place Paul-Painlevé. The building that houses this museum (the **Hôtel de Cluny**) has had many lives. It's been a Roman bathhouse in the 3rd century (you can still visit the ruins downstairs), a mansion for a religious abbot in the 15th century, a royal residence, and, since 1844, a museum. Don't miss the chapel on the second floor. It's a splendid example of flamboyant Gothic architecture.

If you're interested in medieval arts and crafts, you must visit this museum. Chalices, manuscripts, crosses, vestments, carvings, sculptures and the acclaimed *Lady and the Unicorn* tapestries are all here. You enter through the cobblestoned **Cour d'Honneur** (Court of Honor), surrounded by the Gothic building with its gargoyles and turrets. Even if you don't visit the museum, you can visit the beautiful medieval garden.

*Continue down the boulevard St-Michel.*

On your left, you'll see the beautiful fountains in the **place de la Sorbonne**. This is the site of one of the most famous universities in the world. Take a break here at one of the many cafés and soak in the college ambience.

*Return to boulevard St-Michel and continue in the same direction.*

On your right, you'll soon see the black-and-gold fence surrounding the huge **Jardin du Luxembourg** (Luxembourg Gardens), where you'll end your walk. These formal French gardens are referred to as the heart of the Left Bank. Also here is the **Palais du Luxembourg** (Luxembourg Palace), the home of the French Senate, and the **Musée du Luxembourg** (Luxembourg Museum), featuring temporary exhibitions of some of the big names in the history of art.

*You can return to the intersection of boulevard St-Michel and boulevard St-Germain-des-Prés and take the Cluny-La Sorbonne métro back to your hotel.*

## MARAIS WALK
**Approximate distance**: two miles. **Highlights**: Musée Picasso, place des Vosges, and Centre Pompidou.

*Take the métro to the St-Paul stop. When you get out of the métro, you'll be on rue St-Antoine.*

Start walking (east) on the right side of rue St-Antoine until you reach 101, the **Eglise St-Paul-St-Louis**. Stop into this Baroque church with its huge dome dating back to the 1600s. Take a look at the Delacroix painting *Christ on the Mount of Olives* and the shell-shaped holy-water fonts.

*Continue on rue St-Antoine until you reach rue St-Paul. Turn right on rue St-Paul and then turn right at 23/25/27 rue St-Paul.*

You're now in the **Village St-Paul**, an attractive passageway with interesting stores that's known for its antique shops.

*Head back to the intersection of rue St-Paul and rue St-Antoine. Take a right, cross the street at the next crosswalk, and walk to 62 rue St-Antoine.*

Look at the exterior of the **Hôtel Sully**, a mansion in the French Renaissance style and housing **Caisse Nationale des Monuments Historiques**, the headquarters for administering France's historic monuments. Walk into the courtyard and beautiful garden.

*Continue down rue St-Antoine and make a left at rue de Birague.*

You'll now enter the **place des Vosges**, simply the most beautiful square in Paris, in France, and probably in all of Europe. It's the oldest square in the city. It's a beautiful and quiet park surrounded by stone and red-brick houses. Don't miss it! If you want, you can stop at **Maison de Victor Hugo** (Victor Hugo's house), 6 place des Vosges, to view this 19th-century literary legend's home (he wrote *Les Miserables* and *The Hunchback of Notre Dame*).

32 PARIS WALKS

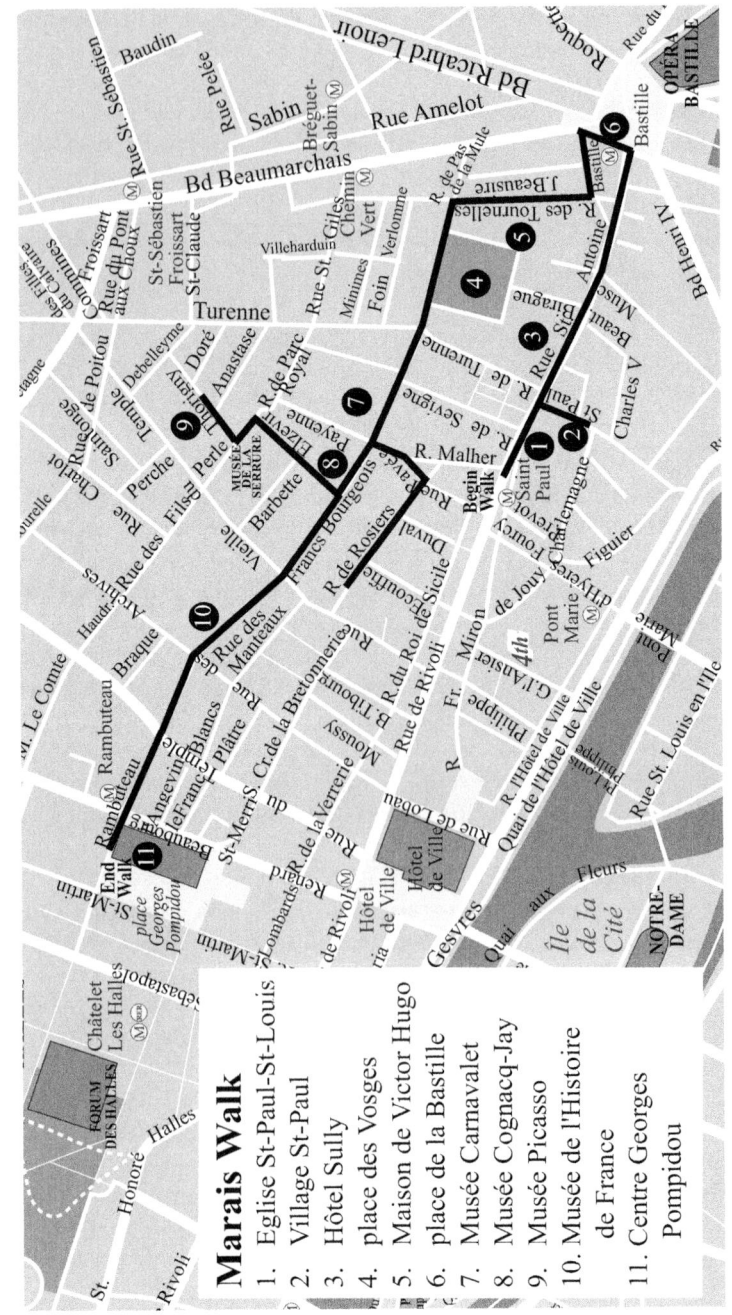

**Marais Walk**
1. Eglise St-Paul-St-Louis
2. Village St-Paul
3. Hôtel Sully
4. place des Vosges
5. Maison de Victor Hugo
6. place de la Bastille
7. Musée Carnavalet
8. Musée Cognacq-Jay
9. Musée Picasso
10. Musée de l'Histoire de France
11. Centre Georges Pompidou

Need a break? Stop in at **Ma Bourgogne,** 19 place des Vosges. This café/restaurant serves traditional Parisian cuisine and specializes in roast chicken. It's a great place for coffee.

*After your break, it's back to rue St-Antoine. Take a left. At the end of rue St-Antoine is a huge traffic roundabout.*

You're now at the **place de la Bastille**. The notorious Bastille prison was torn down over 200 years ago by mobs during the French Revolution. Today, it's a roundabout traffic circle where cars speed around the 170-foot **Colonne de Julliet** (July Column). On the opposite side is the modern **Opéra Bastille**.

This is another opportunity for a break as there are many cafés around the place de la Bastille.

On nearby rue Richard Lenoir (a street off the traffic circle, to your left as you're looking at the July Column), the outdoor **Marché Bastille** market is held every Thursday and Sunday. It's filled with colorful vendors selling everything from stinky cheese to African masks.

*At the end of rue St-Antoine, turn left and walk a short distance and then turn left on rue de la Bastille.*

At 5 rue de la Bastille is **Bofinger**, a beautiful glass-roofed *brasserie*, with lots of stained glass and brass. It's the oldest Alsatian *brasserie* in Paris and still serves traditional dishes like *choucroute* (sauerkraut) and large platters of shellfish. Across the street and less expensive is **Le Petit Bofinger**.

*Turn right from rue de la Bastille onto rue des Tournelles.*

At number 21 is the **Synagogue des Tournelles**. Gustave Eiffel (who designed the extraordinary tower that bears his name) was the engineer of the metal structure of this synagogue.

*Turn left at rue du Pas-de-la-Mule. Continue down rue du Pas-de-la-Mule through the arcades of the place des Vosges. This street turns into the rue des Francs-Bourgeois.*

At the corner of rue des Francs-Bourgeois and rue de Sévigné is the often-overlooked **Musée Carnavalet**. You'll find antiques, portraits and artifacts dating back to the late 1700s in this free museum. The section on the French Revolution with its guillotines is interesting, as is the royal bedroom. There are exhibits across the courtyard at the **Hôtel le Peletier de St-Fargeau**. It's closed on Monday.

### DETOUR
Off of rue des Francs-Bourgeois, you can turn left down rue Pavée and then right onto rue des Rosiers and you find yourself in the heart of **Jewish Paris**. Rue des Rosiers is a great place to get a falafel sandwich and to view shop windows filled with Jewish artifacts. You'll need to retrace your steps back to rue des Francs-Bourgeois.

*Continue on rue des Francs-Bourgeois and make a right on rue Elzévir.*

You'll pass the **Musée Cognacq-Jay** at 8 rue Elzévir. This free museum houses the 18th-century art and furniture collection of the founder of La Samaritaine department store. Works by Rembrandt, Fragonard, Boucher and others are here in this quiet museum housed in the **Hôtel Donon**, an elegant mansion. It's closed on Monday.

*Continue down rue Elzévir. It intersects with rue de Thorigny.*

At 5 rue de Thorigny, you'll find the **Musée Picasso** (don't worry; if you're getting lost, there are signs directing you to the museum). This houses the world's largest collection of the works of Picasso in a 17th-century mansion. It's closed on Tuesday.

*Head back to rue des Francs-Bourgeois.*

At 60 rue des Francs-Bourgeois, you'll find the **Musée de l'Histoire de France/Musée des Archives Nationales**. This museum houses famous French documents, including some written by Joan of Arc, Marie-Antoinette and Napoléon. It's located in the **Hôtel de Clisson**, a palace dating back to 1371, the highlight of which is the incredibly ornate, oval-shaped **Salon Ovale**. It's closed on Tuesday.

*Rue des Francs-Bourgeois becomes rue Rambuteau. As you pass rue du Temple, you'll begin to see your final stop.*

You can't miss the **Centre Georges Pompidou** (a fantastic modern-art museum) at place Georges-Pompidou. The building is a work of art in itself. The controversial building is "ekoskeletal" (all the plumbing, elevators and ducts are exposed and brightly painted). There's a great view from the rooftop restaurant (**Georges**). The museum is closed on Tuesday. Don't miss the **Stravinsky Fountain** with its moving mobile sculptures and circus atmosphere just to the south of the museum. Notice the red pouty lips in the fountain!

After you've had enough of the museum, head right over to the **Café Beaubourg** facing the museum. It's crowded with an artsy crowd and recommended for a drink and perhaps a snack.

*You'll end your walk here and you can take the métro Rambuteau back to your hotel.*

## MAJOR SIGHTS WALK
**Approximate distance**: five miles; two miles to place de l'Alma and three miles to Arc de Triomphe. **Highlights**: Tour Eiffel, Bateaux Mouches, Arc de Triomphe, and Champs-Élysées.

*Take the métro to École Militaire.*

At the métro stop, you'll see the huge **École Militaire** (it's open only on special occasions). This Royal Military Academy was built in the mid-1700s to educate the sons of military officers. The building is a grand example of the French Classical style with its dome and Corinthian pillars. Its most famous alumnus is Napoléon.

*Now start walking toward the Eiffel Tower.*

The **Champ-de-Mars** are the long gardens that stretch from the École Militaire to the **Tour Eiffel** (Eiffel Tower).

It's time to visit one of the most well-known landmarks in the world. It's best to visit the **Tour Eiffel** in either early morning or late evening when the crowds are smaller. Created for the 1889 Universal Exhibition, the Eiffel Tower was built by the same man who designed the framework for the Statue of Liberty. At first it was called, among other things, an "iron monster" when it was erected. Gustave-Alexandre Eiffel never meant for his

7,000-ton tower to be permanent, and it was almost torn down in 1909. Today, it's without doubt the most recognizable structure in the world. Well over 200 million people have visited this monument. You can either take the elevator, or climb the 1,652 stairs.

*Walk behind the Eiffel Tower and cross the bridge (the Pont d'Iéna).*

Once you cross the bridge, you'll be in the **Jardins du Trocadéro** (Trocadéro Gardens), home to the **Palais de Chaillot**. This huge palace, surrounded by more than 60 fountains, was built 80 years ago, and is home to several museums. Also here at the foot of the palace is the **CinéAqua**, a splashy aquarium.

*After taking in the gardens and palace, turn right (as you face the palace and gardens) on the avenue de New York along the Seine River.*

While you're on the avenue de New York, you'll see the **Palais de Tokyo** on the left, a contemporary art center (and one of the most glamorous places for skateboarders).

*Follow avenue de New York until you reach the Pont de l'Alma (the second bridge).*

This bridge, the **Pont de l'Alma**, was created in the time of Napoléon III. The original bridge was replaced in 1972 with the present-day steel structure. Take a look at one of the fanciest high-water markers in the world. Originally, there were four Second Empire soldier statues that decorated the old bridge. Only one, Zouave, remains below the bridge. Parisians use it to measure the height of the water in the Seine. It's said that in 1910, the water reached all the way to Zouave's chin.

You're now at the **place de l'Alma**, one of the most luxurious areas in Paris.

If you have never been in Paris (or for that matter, even if you have), you might want to take a tour of the Seine on the **Bateaux Mouches**. These boats depart from the Right Bank next to the place de l'Alma.

*At the place de l'Alma, you'll see a replica of the torch of the Statue of Liberty.*

38  PARIS WALKS

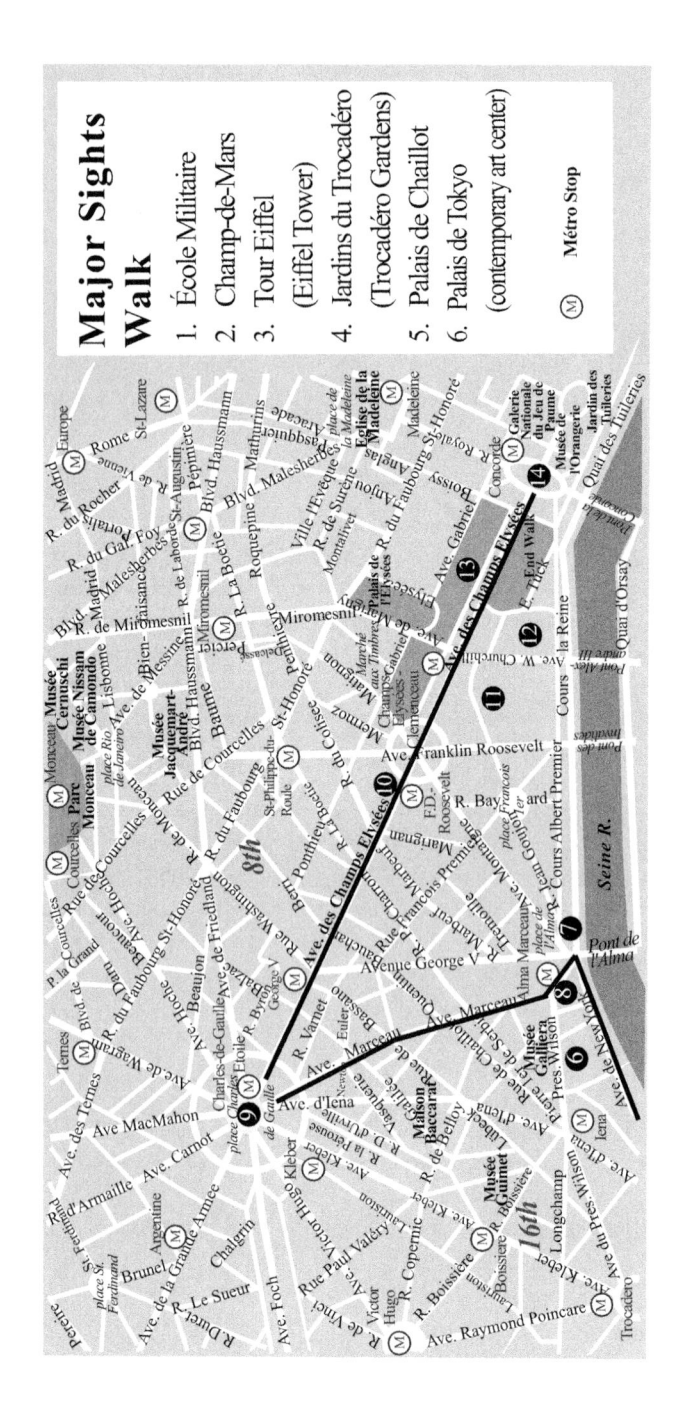

## Major Sights Walk

1. École Militaire
2. Champ-de-Mars
3. Tour Eiffel (Eiffel Tower)
4. Jardins du Trocadéro (Trocadéro Gardens)
5. Palais de Chaillot
6. Palais de Tokyo (contemporary art center)

Ⓜ Métro Stop

WALKS 39

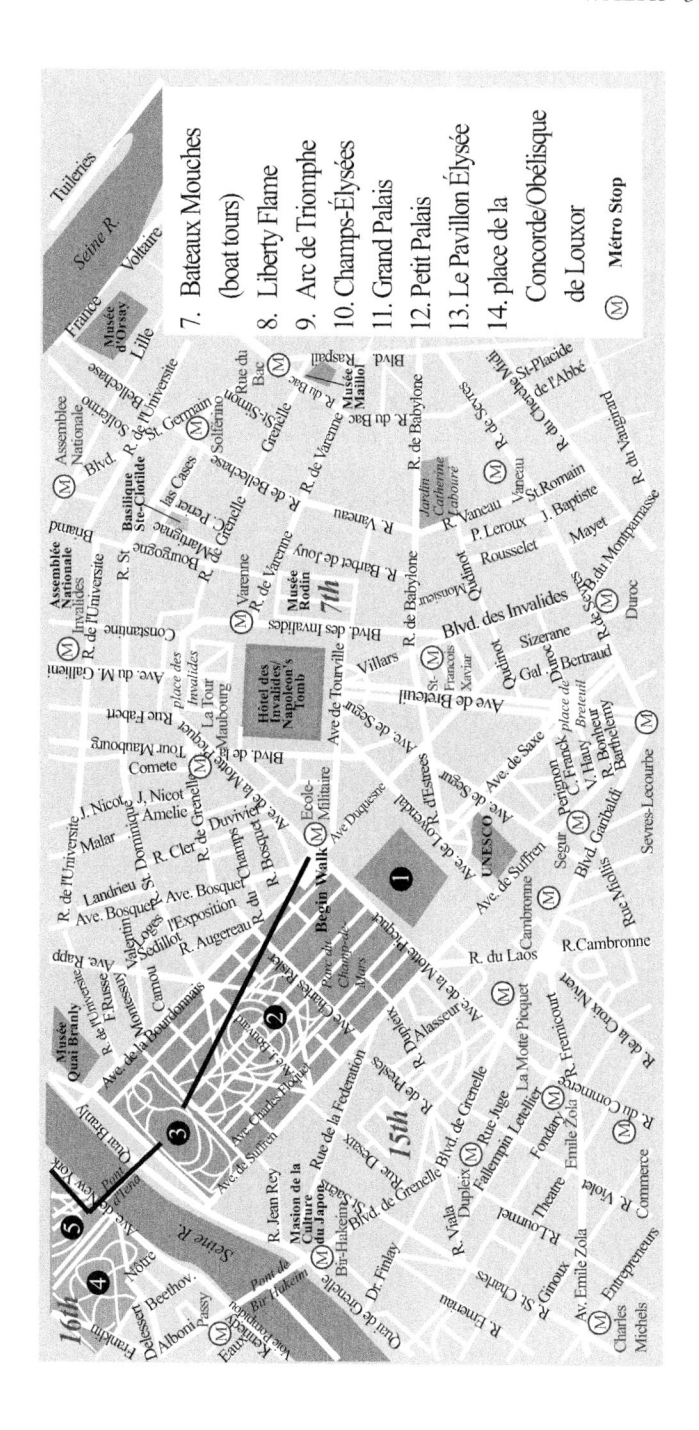

7. Bateaux Mouches (boat tours)
8. Liberty Flame
9. Arc de Triomphe
10. Champs-Élysées
11. Grand Palais
12. Petit Palais
13. Le Pavillon Élysée
14. place de la Concorde/Obélisque de Louxor
Ⓜ Métro Stop

The replica of the torch of the Statue of Liberty was erected here in 1987. It was meant to commemorate the French Resistance during World War II. It just happens to be over the tunnel where Princess Diana and her boyfriend Dodi Al-Fayedh were killed in an automobile crash in 1997. The **Liberty Flame** is now an unofficial shrine covered with notes, flowers and prayers to the dead princess.

*If you've had enough walking, here's a good place to take the métro Alma Marceau back to your hotel. But if you want to continue, head down the avenue Marceau. It's one of the streets off of place de l'Alma. It's about a 10-minute walk on avenue Marceau to the Arc de Triomphe.*

When you get to the **Arc de Triomphe**, don't try to walk across the square. This is Paris's busiest intersection. Twelve avenues pour into the circle around the Arc. There are underground passages, however, that take you to the monument. There's an observation deck providing one of the greatest views of Paris. There's no cost to visit the Arc, but there's an admission fee for the exhibit of photos of the Arc throughout history and for the observation deck. If you aren't impressed by the view down the Champs-Élysées, you really shouldn't have come to Paris.

*Tired? If so, here's a good place to take the métro Charles-de-Gaulle-Étoile back to your hotel. But if you want to continue, head down the Champs-Élysées.*

The left side of the **Champs-Élysées** has more interesting establishments than the banks and businesses on the right side. This street is one of the most famous in the world. It's home to expensive retail shops, fast-food chains, car dealers, banks, huge movie theatres and overpriced cafés. Despite this, you can sit at a café and experience great people-watching (mostly tourists).

On the left side, toward the end of the Champs-Élysées (at number 10) is **Le Pavillon Élysée**, an elegant oblong glass building built for the 1900 World's Fair. It's home to **Lenôtre**, a café and restaurant. A shrine to food in the heart of Paris. Lenôtre's specialty is its desserts, and you can enjoy one with a cup of delicious coffee on the lovely stone terrace that looks onto the gardens.

At avenue Winston-Churchill you can gaze at the recently renovated **Grand** and **Petit Palais**, both built for the 1900 World Exhibition and, like the Eiffel Tower, never meant to be permanent structures. These magnificent buildings remain today in all their glory. The Grand Palais hosts changing art exhibits and the Petit Palais houses the city's fine-arts museum.

*Continue down the Champs-Élysées until you reach the huge place de la Concorde.*

At the end of your walk, admire the huge **place de la Concorde**. In the center of these 21 acres stands the **Obélisque de Louxor** (Obelisk of Luxor), an Egyptian column from the 13th century covered with hieroglyphics. It was moved here in 1833. Now a traffic roundabout, it was here that Louis XVI and Marie-Antoinette were guillotined during the French Revolution.

*You can take the Métro Concorde back to your hotel. The métro stop is at the far left side of the place de la Concorde.*

The **Concorde métro** stop has 44,000 blue-and-white lettered ceramic tiles on its walls. Don't read French? I always wondered if they meant anything. In fact, they do. They spell out the seventeen articles of the declaration of the *Rights of Man and the Citizens* that the French National Assembly adopted in 1789.

## MONTMARTRE WALK

**Approximate distance**: two miles. **Highlights**: Sacré-Coeur, Espace Salvador Dali, and Moulin Rouge. Note: There are lots of steps and steep, cobbled streets on this walk.

*Your walk begins at the Abbesses métro stop.*

This métro stop is the deepest in Paris and stands on the site of a medieval abbey. You'll know this as there are tons of stairs to climb just to get out of the métro. You can also take an elevator to the top.

When you get out of the métro, you'll be at the **place des Abbesses**. Take in the picturesque triangular "square" which features one of the few remaining curvy, green wrought-iron Art Nouveau entrances.

*Off of the place des Abbesses, take rue Yvonne-Le-Tac which becomes rue Tardieu.*

You'll be at the base of the **Basilique du Sacré-Coeur** (Sacred Heart Basilica). It's at the top of the hill (*butte*) and dominates this neighborhood. You can't miss the Basilica with its white onion domes and Byzantine and Romanesque architecture. Completed in 1919, it's named for Christ's sacred heart which some believe is in the crypt. Inside, you'll find gold mosaics, but the real treat is the view of Paris from the dome.

*You have three ways to get to the Basilica. For the price of a métro ticket, you can take the funicular (cable car). You can also take the 224 steps up rue Foyatier (to the left of the cable car) – one of the most photographed sights in Paris – or you can take the steps directly in front of the Basilica.*

If you need a break after visiting the Basilica, stop at the picturesque **Café L'Été en Pente Douce** (which means "summer on a gentle slope") at 23 rue

WALKS 43

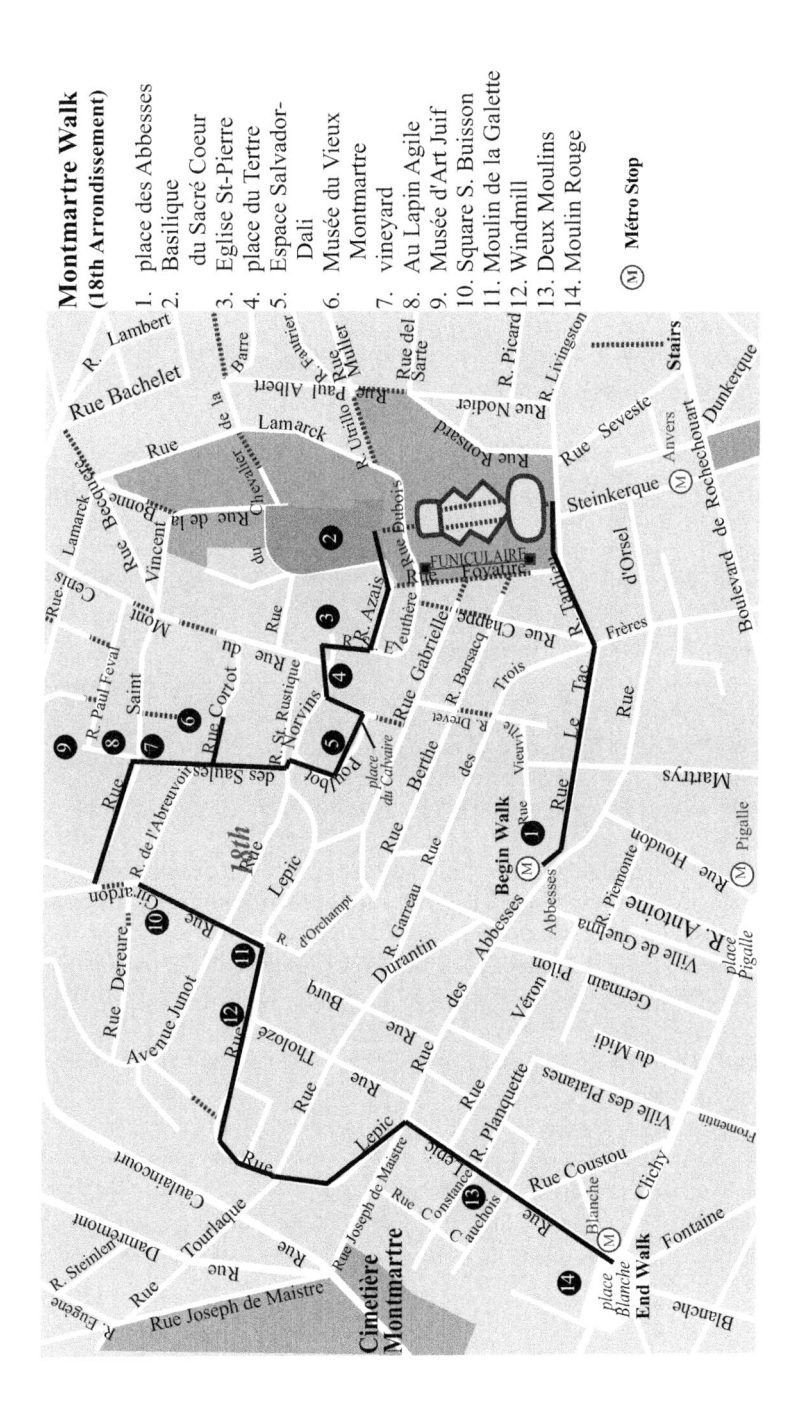

## Montmartre Walk
(18th Arrondissement)

1. place des Abbesses
2. Basilique du Sacré Coeur
3. Eglise St-Pierre
4. place du Tertre
5. Espace Salvador-Dali
6. Musée du Vieux Montmartre
7. vineyard
8. Au Lapin Agile
9. Musée d'Art Juif
10. Square S. Buisson
11. Moulin de la Galette
12. Windmill
13. Deux Moulins
14. Moulin Rouge

Ⓜ Métro Stop

Muller. If you're facing the Basilica, take the steps down to your right (rue Maurice-Utrillo) and at the bottom is rue Muller and the café.

*With the Basilica to your back, turn to the right and follow rue Azaïs and then take a right onto rue St-Eleuthère.*

On your right will be the **Eglise St-Pierre**, one of the oldest churches in Paris. The Roman marble columns date back to the 1100s.

*Head down rue Norvins (it's to your left with the Eglise St-Pierre to your back) through the place du Tertre.*

The attractive **place du Tertre** is overrun with tourists and artists trying to paint your portrait. There's a circus-like atmosphere here.

*Across the square is the short rue du Calvaire. Turn right into the place du Calvaire (right before you reach the stairs heading down the hill).*

On the other side of this attractive square is our next stop, **Espace Salvador-Dali**, at 11 rue Poulbot. Black walls, weird music with Dali's voice and dim lighting all make this museum an interesting experience. Come here if you're a fan of Salvador Dali to see 300 of his lithographs and etchings and 25 sculptures.

*Continue on rue Poulbot, make a left on rue Norvins and a quick right down rue des Saules.*

You can take a right onto beautiful rue Cortot to visit the **Musée du Vieux Montmartre** at 12 rue Cortot. Renoir and van Gogh are just a couple of the artists who have occupied this 17th-century house. It now has a collection of mementos of the neighborhood, including paintings, posters and photographs.

*If you don't visit the museum, continue down rue des Saules.*

On your right is the last remaining **vineyard** in Paris at the corner of rue St-Vincent and rue des Saules near the place Jules Joffrin. They still sell wine here. The labels are designed by local artists. The harvesting of the grapes in October gives the residents of Montmartre yet another excuse to have a festival.

You'll likely hear French folk tunes coming out of the shuttered cottage at the picturesque intersection of rue des Saules and rue St-Vincent. **Au Lapin Agile/Cabaret des Assassins** was once frequented by Picasso. Today, you'll sit at small wooden tables and listen to *chansonniers* (singers). A truly Parisian experience.

If you're interested in ancient and modern Jewish art, you can continue down the many stairs of rue des Saules to the **Musée d'Art Juif** at 42 rue des Saules. It's closed Friday, Saturday and August.

*Turn left on rue St-Vincent and make a left at place Constantine Pecquer. Climb the stairs (yes, more stairs!). At the top is rue Girardon.*

The park on your right is **Square Suzanne Buisson**, named after a leader of the French Resistance. According to legend, St-Denis (after being decapitated) carried his head here and washed it in the fountain. There's a statue of him holding his head.

*Follow rue Girardon until you reach the corner of rue Lepic.*

In the 19th century, Montmartre had many vineyards and over 40 windmills. One of the two surviving windmills, the **Moulin de la Galette**, is on this corner. If it looks familiar, it's the windmill depicted by Renoir in his painting of the same name. It's now part of a restaurant.

*From here turn right on rue Lepic.*

You'll see the other surviving **windmill** on your right at the corner of rue Tholozé.

*Continue downhill (finally!) on rue Lepic.*

Van Gogh lived at 54 rue Lepic in 1886.

The movie *Amélie* won not only many film awards, but also a cult following. The lead character is a waitress. You can visit Amélie's 1950s bistro **Bar-tabac des Deux Moulins** at 15 rue Lepic, 18th/Métro Blanche, where you'll find mostly locals enjoying good homemade desserts and standard bistro fare.

*At the end of rue Lepic at place Blanche, turn right onto boulevard de Clichy.*

At 82 boulevard de Clichy, you'll see the **Moulin Rouge**. Originally a red windmill, this dance hall has been around since 1889. It's without a doubt the most famous cabaret in the world. Toulouse-Lautrec memorialized the Moulin Rouge in his paintings, and it got a boost in business from the more recent movie of the same name. Looking for a little bit of Vegas? You'll find it here.

*Here, you can head home at the métro Blanche stop (especially if you have kids with you), or you can head left (with the Moulin Rouge to your back) down boulevard de Clichy to place Pigalle.*

You come to **place Pigalle** for only one thing: sex. Littered with sex shops, this area was known as "Pig Alley" during World War II.

*You can end your trip here at the métro Pigalle stop.*

## CULINARY WALKS

**Approximate distance**: a quarter of a mile. **Highlights**: Lavinia (wine shop) and Fauchon (culinary souvenirs). Note that most are closed on Sunday.

This short walk is packed with specialty-food shops, wine dealers, restaurants, and tea rooms.

*Take the métro to the Madeleine stop. Your walk begins at the place de la Madeleine in the 8th. Begin at Lavinia and continue around the square.*

- **Boutique Maille** *(number 6 place de la Madeleine)*. Boutique mustard shop.

- **Caviar Kaspia** *(number 17)*. Caviar, blinis and salmon. There's also a restaurant upstairs.

- **Nicolas** *(number 31)*. Located upstairs from the Nicolas wine shop. You can buy a bottle of wine at the shop and have it served with your meal. The menu is limited, but the wines sold by the glass are inexpensive.

- **Fauchon** *(number 30)*. Deli and grocery known for its huge selection of canned food, baked goods and alcohol. The store is a must for those wanting to bring back French specialties.

- **La Maison du Miel** *(located around the corner from Fauchon at 24 rue Vignon)*. This food store contains everything made from honey (from sweets to soap).

- **Lavinia** *(number 3-5 boulevard de la Madeleine)*. The largest wine shop in Paris with wines priced from 3 to 3,600 euros. Drink any bottle from the shop at the wine bar. Lunch served—with wine, of course.

There are several areas in Paris where many **restaurants are concentrated in small pockets**:

- **Rue Pot-de-Fer** between la rue Tournefort and la rue Mouffetard, just off the market. (5th/Métro Monge).

- **Passage Brady** (enter around 33 boulevard de Strasbourg) with inexpensive Indian, Turkish, and Moroccan restaurants.(10th/Métro Château d'Eau).

- **Place Ste-Catherine** (enter from rue Caron off of rue St-Antoine) in the Marais. Seven restaurants are located on this lovely square. Tel. 01/42.72.37.21. (4th/Métro St-Paul).

- **Off of la rue St-Jacques** in the area around la rue St-Séverin and la rue de la Huchette for French, Italian, Greek and other touristy restaurants jammed into small streets. (5th/Métro St-Michel).

## PARISIAN MARKETS

It is worth a trip to see a real **outdoor Parisian market**. Filled with colorful vendors, stinky cheese, fresh produce, poultry and hanging rabbits, this is real Paris at its most diverse and beautiful. Parisians still shop (some every day) at food markets around the city. Unless noted otherwise, all are open Tuesday through noon on Sunday. Some of the best-known are:

**Rue Montorgueil**, 1st/Métro Les Halles
**Rue Mouffetard**, 5th/Métro Censier-Daubenton
**Rue de Buci**, 6th/Métro Mabillon
**Marché Raspail** on boulevard Raspail, 6th/Métro Rennes (open Sunday) (organic)
**Rue Cler**, 7th/Métro École Militaire
**Marché Bastille** on the boulevard Richard Lenoir, 11th/Métro Bastille (open Thursday and Sunday)
**Rue Daguerre**, 14th/Métro Denfert-Rochereau
**Rue Poncelet**, 17th/Métro Ternes

## 5. Practical Matters

**GETTING TO PARIS**
Airports/Arrival
Paris has two international airports: **Charles de Gaulle** (**Roissy**) and **Orly**. **Orly** has two terminals: Sud (south) for international flights, and Ouest (west) for domestic flights. A free shuttle bus connects the two.

At Charles de Gaulle, a free shuttle bus connects **Aérogare 1** (used by most foreign carriers) with **Aérogare 2** (used primarily by Air France). This bus also drops you off at the Roissy train station. You can also walk through the terminals to the train station (just follow the signs). Once you get to the train station, you can use the self-service ticket kiosks (with instructions in English) or get in line at the ticket office. Your ticket is good for a transfer from the train to the metro system. Line RER B departs every 15 minutes from 5:30am to midnight to major métro stations. The cost is €10.30. Connecting métro lines will take you to your final destination. The train stops at Gare du Nord, Châtelet-Les Halles, St-Michel and Luxembourg stations. The trip takes about 35 minutes to Châtelet-Les Halles. By the way, keep your ticket. You need it to enter and exit the train stations.

The **Roissy buses** run every 15 minutes (from 6am-10:30pm) to and from the bus stop at Opéra Garnier on rue Scribe. (€13.20, about a one-hour trip). You can reach your final destination by taking the métro from the nearby Opéra métro station.

The cost of a **taxi** ride from CDG is fixed at least €50 to the Left Bank and €55 to the Right Bank. A taxi from Orly is €30 to the Left Bank and €35 to the Right Bank. Drivers are allowed to charge €4 for each additional rider. You'll find the taxi line outside the terminals. It will frequently be long, but moves quite fast. Never take an unmetered taxi!

Minivan shuttles cost from €15 per person (shared ride). One service is **Parishuttle**, www.paris-shuttle.com, Tel. 1 877 404-9674 (from the US and Canada).

## GETTING AROUND PARIS
**Car Rental**
Are you crazy? Parking is chaotic, gas is extremely expensive, and driving in Paris is an unpleasant "adventure." With the incredible public transportation system in Paris, there's absolutely no reason to rent a car. If you do intend to drive, all major car rental companies have offices at both airports.

**Métro (Subway)**
The métro system is clearly the best way to get around Paris. It's orderly, inexpensive and for the most part safe. You're rarely far follow the line that your stop is on and note the last stop (the last stop appears on all the signs) and you'll soon be scurrying about underground like a Parisian. Service starts at 5:20am and ends at 12:40am (one additional hour on Saturday night/Sunday mornings and the eve of holidays). Métro tickets are also valid on buses. Each ticket costs €1.90. Buy a *carnet* (10 tickets for €14.90). www.ratp.fr. Some métro stations have information desks and most have machines where you can purchase your tickets (and most machines have instructions in English). A day pass is €7.50.

If you're staying in Paris for a longer period of time, a *carte navigo* for zones 1 and 2 (Paris and nearby suburbs) costs about €22 (plus a one-time fee of €5) a week. This pass is valid for travel from Monday to Sunday, rather than a continuous seven day period, which makes it less attractive for visitors arriving mid-week. The pass allows unlimited use of both the métro and the bus system. You'll need a pass (you can get them at any major métro station) and a passport-size photo. That's why there are so many of those photo booths at stations. There are many options available for métro passes. Check them out. Keep your ticket throughout your trip. An inspector can fine you if you can't produce a stamped ticket.

**Buses**
Buses run from 5:30am to midnight, with some night routes running through the night. Bus routes are shown on the *Plan des Autobus*, a map available at métro stations. The route is shown at each bus stop. **You can use métro tickets on the bus**, but you can't switch between the bus and métro on the same ticket. Enter through the front door and validate your ticket in the machine behind the driver. You can also purchase a ticket from the driver. Exit out the back door. Each ticket costs €1.90 (€2 if bought on the bus).

If you'd like a quick tour of major sights, **bus #69** will take you from the Eiffel Tower (**bus stop: Rapp-La Bourdonnais**) passing the Seine River, the Louvre, through the Marais all the way to Père Lachaise Cemetery.

**Taxis/Uber**
You'll pay a minimum of €5 for a taxi ride. Fares are usually described in English on a sticker on the window. A typical 10-minute ride will cost around €10. There are taxi stands around the city, often near métro stops. **Taxis G7** has a dedicated line for requests in English. Call 01/41.27.66.99. **Uber** is also widely available in Paris.

## BASIC INFORMATION
**Banking & Changing Money**
The **euro (€)** is the currency of France and most of Europe. Before you leave for Paris, it's a good idea to get some euros. It makes your arrival a lot easier. Call your credit-card company or bank before you leave to tell them that you'll be using your ATM or credit card outside the country. Many have automatic controls that can "freeze" your account if the computer program determines that there are charges outside your normal area. ATMs (of course, with fees) are the easiest way to change money in Paris. You'll find them everywhere. You can still get traveler's checks, but why bother? Many places no longer accept traveler's checks due to counterfeit checks.

**Business Hours**
Shop hours vary, but generally are from 9:30am to 7:30pm from Monday through Saturday. Most shops are closed on Sunday. Many restaurants and

shops close for the month of August.

### Climate & Weather
Average high temperature/low temperature/days of rain:
- January: 43º F / 34º F / 10
- February: 45º / 34º / 9
- March: 51º / 38º / 10
- April: 57º / 42º / 9
- May: 64º / 48º/ 10
- June: 70º /54º / 9
- July: 75º/ 58º / 8
- August: 75º / 57º / 7
- September: 69º / 52º / 9
- October: 59º / 46º / 10
- November: 49º / 39º / 10
- December: 45º / 36º / 11

Check www.weather.com before you leave.

### Consulates & Embassies
- **US**: 8th/Métro Concorde, 2 ave. Gabriel, Tel. 01/43.12.22.22
- **Canada**: 8th/Métro Franklin-D. Roosevelt, 35 avenue Montaigne, Tel. 01/44.43.29.00

### Electricity
The electrical current in Paris is 220 volts as opposed to 110 volts found at home. Don't fry your electric razor, hairdryer or laptop. You'll need a converter and an adapter. (Most laptops don't require a converter, but why are you bringing that anyway?)

### Emergencies & Safety
Paris is one of the safest large cities in the world. Still, don't wear a "fanny pack;" it's a sign that you're a tourist and an easy target (especially in crowded tourist areas and the métro). Avoid wearing expensive jewelry in the métro.

### Insurance
Check with your health-care provider. Most policies don't cover you overseas. If that's the case, you may want to obtain medical insurance. Given the uncertainties in today's world, you may also want to purchase trip-cancellation insurance (for insurance coverage, check out www.insuremytrip.com). Make sure that your policy covers sickness, disasters, bankruptcy and State Depart-

ment travel restrictions and warnings. In other words, read the fine print!

**Festivals**
**January**: If you love shopping, it's time for post-holiday bargains. Parisians call it "*les soldes*." Paris is also host to the international ready-to-wear fashion shows held at the Parc des Expositions (15th).

**February**: The *Salon de l'Agriculture* showcases France's important agricultural industry. Included in the celebration are food and wine from throughout France.

**March:** At the end of the month is the *Foire du Trône*, a huge amusement park held at the Bois de Vincennes (12th). With Ferris wheels, circus attractions and carousels, it's like a sophisticated county fair.

**April**: Paris is home to the International Marathon. On the first weekend, spectators line the Champs-Élysées to watch the women's and men's marathons. Events and concerts featuring jazz artists are held throughout the city.

**May**: Tennis is king in late May as Paris hosts the French Open (they call it "*Roland Garros*").

**June**: Music fills the air during the many concerts as part of the *Fête de la Musique*. From Guatemalan street musicians to serious opera, you'll be exposed to Paris's diversity. Most concerts are free. Some of the best jazz artists come to Paris in June and July for the Paris Jazz Fest. Events and concerts are held in the Parc Floral (Bois de Vincennes).

**July**: In early July, Paris hosts a huge gay-pride parade. On the 14th, Parisians celebrate *Le Quatorze Juillet* or Bastille Day (*see photo at left*) with city-wide celebrations, fireworks and a huge military parade down the Champs-Élysées. In late July, the

*Tour de France* is completed when bikers ride down the Champs-Élysées. This is also a huge month for *soldes* (clothing sales).

**August**: Sunbathe, drink and celebrate the Seine River at *Paris-Plage*. Hundreds of deck chairs, umbrellas, cabanas and even palm trees are all brought to the Right Bank of the river from Pont de Sully to Pont Neuf. You can enjoy the sun, have a drink or two and a snack. No, I don't recommend that you swim in the Seine. In the late afternoon and evening, musicians play along the river.

**September**: You can visit historical monuments (some of which are usually closed to the public) during *Fête du Patrimoine*. In late September, Paris again hosts the international ready-to-wear fashion convention at Parc des Expositions (15th).

**October**: Thousands of horse-racing fans arrive in Paris for the *Prix de l'Arc de Triomphe Lucien Barrière*. It's considered to be the ultimate thoroughbred horse race. It's held at the Hippodrome de Longchamps (16th).

**November**: Only in France would the arrival of wine be celebrated as a huge event. Get ready to drink **Beaujolais Nouveau** (a fruity wine from Burgundy) on the third Thursday.

**December**: A skating rink is installed in front of the **Hôtel de Ville** (City Hall). The large windows of the major department stores (Bon Marché, BHV, Galeries Lafayette and Printemps) are decorated in interesting (sometimes bizarre) Christmas themes. *Fête de St-Sylvestre* (New Year's Eve) is celebrated throughout the city. At midnight, the Eiffel Tower is a virtual light show and the city is filled with champagne-drinking Parisians welcoming the new year (and a few tourists hoping they'll return to this great city in the years to come).

### Holidays
- **New Year's:** January 1
- **Easter**
- **Ascension** (40 days after Easter)
- **Pentecost** (seventh Sunday after Easter)
- **May Day:** May 1
- **Victory in Europe:** May 8
- **Bastille Day:** July 14

- **Assumption of the Virgin Mary**: August 15
- **All Saints'**: November 1
- **Armistice**: November 11
- **Christmas**: December 25

### Internet Access

Cyber cafés seem to pop up everywhere (and go out of business quickly). You shouldn't have difficulty finding a place to e-mail home. The going rate is about €3 per hour. WiFi is available at many bars, cafes, and restaurants.

### Language

Please, make the effort to speak a little French. It will get you a long way — even if all you can say is *Parlez-vous anglais?* (par-lay voo ahn-glay): Do you speak English? Gone are the days when Parisians were only interested in correcting your French. You'll find helpful French phrases in a few pages.

### Packing

Never pack prescription drugs, eyeglasses or valuables. Carry them on. Think black. It always works for men and women. Oh, and by the way, pack light. Don't ruin your trip by having to lug around huge suitcases. Before you leave home, make copies of your passport, airline tickets and confirmation of hotel reservations. You should also make a list of your credit-card numbers and the telephone numbers for your credit-card companies. If you lose any of them (or they're stolen), you can call someone at home and have them provide the information to you. You should also pack copies of these documents separate from the originals.

### Passport Regulations

You'll need a **valid passport** to enter France. If you're staying more than 90 days, you must obtain a visa. Canadians don't need visas.

Citizens of the U.S. who have been away more than 48 hours can bring home $800 of merchandise duty-free every 30 days. For more information, go to Traveler Information ("Know Before You Go") at www.cbp.gov. Canadians can bring back C$800 each year if gone for 48 hours or more. For more information for Canadians, visit travel.gc.ca.

Hotel and restaurant prices are required by law to include taxes and service charges. **Value Added Tax** (VAT, or TVA in France) is nearly 20% (higher on luxury goods). The VAT is included in the price of goods (except services such as restaurants). Foreigners are entitled to a refund and must fill out a refund form. When you make your purchase, ask for the form and instructions if you're purchasing €175 or more in one place and in one day (no combining). Yes, it can be a hassle. Check out www.global-blue.com or www.premiertaxfree.com for the latest information on refunds (and help for a fee).

### Postal Services
Be prepared to wait in line. A main post office at 16 rue Etienne-Marcel is open daily. If you're mailing postcards, you can purchase stamps at many *tabacs* (tobacco shops) and stands that sell newspapers and postcards.

### Restrooms
There aren't a lot of public restrooms. If you need to go, your best bet is to head (no pun intended) to the nearest café or brasserie. It's considered good manners to purchase something if you use the restroom. Some métro stations have public restrooms. Another option are those strange self-cleaning restrooms that look like some sort of pod found on some streets in Paris (they are free). Don't be shocked to walk into a restroom and find two porcelain foot prints and a hole in the floor. A few of these old "Turkish toilets" still exist. Hope you have strong thighs!

### Smoking
There is a smoking ban for all public places. Beginning in 2008, restaurants, hotels, bars-tabacs, and nightclubs must be smoke-free. If it can happen in Paris, it can happen anywhere. You can still smoke at outdoor cafés.

### Telephones
- Country code for France is 33
- Area code for Paris is 01
- Calls beginning with 0800 are toll-free
- Calling Paris from the U.S. and Canada: dial 011-33-1 plus the eight-digit local number. You drop the 0 in the area code
- Calling the U.S. or Canada from Paris: dial 00 (wait for the tone), dial 1 plus the area code and local number
- Calling within Paris: dial 01 and the eight-digit local number.

**Phone cards** are the cheapest way to call. Get one from many *tabacs* or magazine kiosks.

A great way to stay in touch and save money is to **rent an international cell phone**. One provider is www.cellhire.com. Few cell phones purchased in the U.S. work in Europe. If you're a frequent visitor to Europe, you may want to purchase a cell phone (for about $50) from www.mobal.com. You'll get an international telephone number and pay by the minute for calls made on your cell phone. If you are using a smartphone in Paris, make sure to turn off your international roaming (and use WiFi instead) to save money.

### Time
When it's noon in New York City, it's 6pm in Paris. For hours of events or schedules, the French use the 24-hour clock. So 6am is 0600 and 1pm is 1300.

### Tipping
Restaurants: A service charge is almost always added to your bill in Paris. Most locals round up to the next euro and it's okay if that is what you do, too. Travelers from the U.S. sometimes have trouble not tipping. Remember, you do *not* have to tip. The menu will usually note that service is included (*service compris*). Sometimes this is abbreviated with the letters s.c. The letters s.n.c. stand for *service non compris*; this means that the service is not included in the price, and you must leave a tip. This is extremely rare. You will sometimes find *couvert* or cover charge on your menu (a small charge just for placing your butt at the table). Other tips: round up to the next euro for taxi drivers, €1 per bag to the hotel porter, and €.50 to €1 for bathroom attendants.

## Tourist Information
There are tourist information offices at both airports. The main tourist office is located at **25 rue des Pyramides** (1st/Métro Pyramides): Open daily 9am-7pm (winter 10am-7pm). Closed May 1.

## Water
Tap water is safe in Paris. Occasionally, you'll find *non potable* signs in restrooms. This means that the water is not safe for drinking.

## Web Sites
- Paris Tourist Office: www.parisinfo.com
- French Government Tourist Office: us.france.fr
- U.S. State Department: www.state.gov

## ESSENTIAL FRENCH PHRASES
please, *s'il vous plaît* (seel voo *play*)
thank you, *merci* (*mair* see)
yes, *oui* (wee)
no, *non* (nohn)
good morning, *bonjour* (bohn *jhoor*)
good afternoon, *bonjour* (bohn *jhoor*)
good evening, *bonsoir* (bohn *swahr*)
goodbye, *au revoir* (o ruh *vwahr*)
sorry/excuse me, *pardon* (pahr-*dohn*)
you are welcome, *de rien* (duh ree *ehn*)

do you speak English?, *parlez-vous anglais?* (par lay voo ahn *glay*)
I don't speak French, *je ne parle pas français* (jhuh ne parl pah frahn *say*)
I don't understand, *je ne comprends pas* (jhuh ne kohm *prahn* pas)
I'd like a table, *je voudrais une table* (zhuh voo *dray* ewn tabl)
I'd like to reserve a table, *je voudrais réserver une table* (zhuh voo *dray* rayzehrvay ewn tabl)
for one, *pour un* (poor oon), two, *deux* (duh), *trois* (twah)(3), *quatre* (kaht-ruh)(4), *cinq* (sank)(5), *six* (cease)(6), *sept* (set)(7), *huit* (wheat)(8), *neuf* (nerf)(9), *dix* (dease)(10)
waiter/sir, *monsieur* (muh-*syuh*) (never *garçon*!)
waitress/miss, *mademoiselle* (mad mwa *zel*)
knife, *couteau* (koo *toe*)
spoon, *cuillère* (kwee *air*)
fork, *fourchette* (four *shet*)

menu, *la carte* (la cart) (not *menu*!)
wine list, *la carte des vins* (la *cart* day van)
no smoking, *défense de fumer* (day *fahns* de fu may)
toilets, *les toilettes* (lay twa *lets*)

closed, *fermé* (fehr-may)
open, *ouvert* (oo-vehr)
today, *aujourd'hui* (o zhoor *dwee*)
tomorrow, *demain* (duh *mehn*)
tonight, *ce soir* (suh *swahr*)
Monday, *lundi* (luhn *dee*)
Tuesday, *mardi* (mahr *dee*)
Wednesday, *mercredi* (mair kruh *dee*)
Thursday, *jeudi* (jheu *dee*)
Friday, *vendredi* (vawn druh *dee*)
Saturday, *samedi* (sahm *dee*)
Sunday, *dimanche* (dee *mahnsh*)

here, *ici* (ee-*see*)
there, *là* (la)
what, *quoi* (kwah)
when, *quand* (kahn)
where, *où est* (ooh-eh)
how much, *c'est combien* (say comb bee *ehn*)
credit cards, *les cartes de crédit* (lay kart duh creh *dee*)

**UPDATES**

Updates to this guide can be found on the blog at *www.eatndrink.com*.

**ACKNOWLEDGMENTS**

French editor: Marie Fossier
English editor: Marian Modesta Olson
Website: www.eatndrink.com
Contributor: Karl Raaum
Additional research: Mark Berry, Terrie Cooper, Christine Humphrey, Jeff Kurz, Trish Medalen, Terry Medalen, Gay Miller, Jon Miller, Jim Mortell, and Dan Schmidt.

All photos from Shutterstock, pixabay.com and Karl Raaum.
Front cover image: Benh LIEU SONG (wikimedia images).

Note: the use of these photos does not represent an endorsement of this book or any services listed within by any of the photographers listed above.

For a list of all Europe Made Easy travel guides, and to purchase our books, visit **www.eatndrink.com**

*Informative, Opinionated, Funny.*

The best menu translator/restaurant guides available!
Handy, pocket-sized ... a must for all travelers.

Check out other guides published by Europe Made Easy!

Europe, Paris, Berlin, Barcelona, and Amsterdam
Made Easy.

www.eatndrink.com